A BASIC BOOK OF
RABBITS
LOOK-AND-LEARN

BY
MARCY MYEROVICH

Front cover photo of a Dutch rabbit by Ray Hanson.

Back cover photos of Netherland Dwarf rabbits by Isabelle Francais and Michael Gilroy; photos of Mini Rex rabbits by Isabelle Francais.

Distributed in the UNITED STATES to the Pet Trade by T.F.H. Publications, Inc., One T.F.H. Plaza, Neptune City, NJ 07753; distributed in the UNITED STATES to the Bookstore and Library Trade by National Book Network, Inc. 4720 Boston Way, Lanham MD 20706; in CANADA to the Pet Trade by H & L Pet Supplies Inc., 27 Kingston Crescent, Kitchener, Ontario N2B 2T6; Rolf C. Hagen Ltd., 3225 Sartelon Street, Montreal 382 Quebec; in CANADA to the Book Trade by Macmillan of Canada (A Division of Canada Publishing Corporation), 164 Commander Boulevard, Agincourt, Ontario M1S 3C7; in the United Kingdom by T.F.H. Publications, PO Box 15, Waterlooville PO7 6BQ; in AUSTRALIA AND THE SOUTH PACIFIC by T.F.H. (Australia), Pty. Ltd., Box 149, Brookvale 2100 N.S.W., Australia; in NEW ZEALAND by Brooklands Aquarium Ltd. 5 McGiven Drive, New Plymouth, RD1 New Zealand; in Japan by T.F.H. Publications, Japan—Jiro Tsuda, 10-12-3 Ohjidai, Sakura, Chiba 285, Japan; in SOUTH AFRICA by Multipet Pty. Ltd., P.O. Box 35347, Northway, 4065, South Africa. Published by T.F.H. Publications, Inc.

Manufactured in the United States of America by T.F.H. Publications, Inc.

RABBIT BOOKS FROM T.F.H.

T.F.H. offers the most comprehensive selection of books dealing with rabbits. A selection of significant titles is presented below; they and many other works are available from your local pet shop.

TT-003, 96 pgs, 118 color photos

PB-724, 80 pgs, 46 color photos

KW-021, 128 pgs, 127 color photos

J-001, 48 pgs, 33 color photos

CO-0225, 128 pgs, 95 color photos

TW-121, 256 pgs, 109 color photos

H-1073, 128 pgs, 76 color photos

H-984, 320 pgs, 231 color photos

PS-809, 128 pgs, 90 color photos

PS-796, 112 pgs, 75 color photos

SK-001, 64 pgs, 43 color photos

YF-114, 32 pgs, 16 color photos

M-543, 96 pgs, 30 color photos

T-107, 64 pgs, 40 color photos

E-724, 32 pgs

Contents

INTRODUCTION 4

SELECTION 8

HOUSING 16

CARE 22

DIET 26

HEALTH 34

REGULAR RABBITS 38

WOOLY RABBITS 56

THE LITTLEST ONES 60

Dedicated to Daffodil and Mopsy

Photography: Isabelle Francais, Michael Gilroy, Ray Hanson, Michael Mettler, Susan C. Miller, David Robinson, Vince Serbin, and Louise Van der Meid.

INTRODUCTION

All of the kinds of pet rabbit that we know today are descended from the European, or common, wild rabbit, who bears the scientific name *Oryctolagus cuniculus.* For many years, rabbits were ranked within the animal order known as Rodentia, which includes those mammals that most people know as rodents: rats, mice, and hamsters, to name just a few. However, even though rabbits and rodents share the characteristic of teeth that grow continuously, scientists have determined that the relationship between the two groups of animals is not nearly as close as originally thought to be.

◀ Rabbits have also played a significant role in folklore and literature. In Europe especially they are associated with the coming of spring, and for many generations children have been charmed by the adventures of beloved bunny rabbits such as Beatrix Potter's Peter Rabbit.

Thus, rabbits today are placed within an order of their own, which is known as the order Lagomorpha.

In spite of the odds against them caused by famine, disease, and predators, rabbits have long proved to be hardy, adaptable animals. Additionally, because they are such prolific breeders, their population in the wild remains at a fairly constant level, unless man intervenes. ➥

◀ Netherland Dwarf. It is likely that the Romans were the first to breed rabbits as a source of food. They domesticated rabbits by keeping them within gardens protected by walls of stone. Today, the rabbit still figures prominently in the production of meat for human consumption.

INTRODUCTION

American Fuzzy ▶
Lops. There are over
40 breeds of rabbit,
and they range in
size from two to
over fourteen
pounds. Some
breeds were initially
developed for a specific reason, such as for the production of
meat or pelts. Today, a sizable number of breeds exist that serve
for the purpose of
exhibition or
as family
pets.

◀ Today, small rabbits like
these Netherland Dwarfs are
among the most popular
breeds of rabbit. They do not
require a great deal of space
and can thus be kept even by
those people who live in
small apartments.

▲ Rabbits are
interesting pets
because they are
curious about
their
environment and
respond quickly
to stimuli.

INTRODUCTION

It is theorized that rabbits were first domesticated in Spain. Their spread throughout other areas of Europe was brought about in part by the Phoenicians, who included rabbits among their items of trade. At a later point in time, the Romans discovered the rabbit as a valuable food commodity, and Roman armies helped to broaden the range of the species as they moved throughout their travels.

The rabbit fancy as we know it today had its actual beginnings sometime later than this: by about the l4th century, when French monks began writing up accounts of selective breeding. Their efforts meant that larger "meat" (used for food) rabbits could be produced and that new colors could be developed.

American Fuzzy Lop. Rabbits are cute, and rabbits are cuddly—just a few of many reasons why they are desirable as pets.

A family of Mini Rex. Rabbits are popular pets because— among other things—they are very easy to tame. ▶

A Dutch rabbit. The hallmark of this breed is the distinctive bi-color pattern. In a good specimen, the markings should be clearly delineated.

◀ The smaller dwarf-like rabbit breeds are essentially just as hardy as their bigger brothers.

▶ A Polish rabbit being placed into its travel cage. Cages made of wire are a good investment. They are less subject to damage caused by a rabbit's gnawing or urine build-up.

◀ Rabbits have many advantages as pets. Unlike many other household pets, rabbits make no noise and do not give off unpleasant odors if they are cared for properly.

▶ A family of Himalayan-marked rabbits. This is a well-known color pattern that is also found in some other kinds of animals. In Himalayan rabbits, the markings on the ears, nose, feet, and tail may be in one of two colors: black or blue.

SELECTION

The biggest decision that you will have to make when selecting your pet rabbit is in choosing a breed that will be suitable for you and your family. Naturally, personal preference will play a big part, but there are several factors that must be considered before you make your final choice. First, think about size. If you are thinking about a rabbit such as the New Zealand, whose weight can range from nine to eleven pounds, will young members of the family be able to comfortably handle the animal? Do you have ample room for accommodations for a rabbit of this size?

➤ Netherland Dwarfs. In the majority of breeds of rabbit, there are a number of colors available.

➤ A playful pair of lop-eared rabbits. Be sure to observe how your prospective pet moves around in its environment. A healthy rabbit will be able to hippity-hop around without limping or faltering.

➤ Jersey Wooly. This is one of the newer breeds of rabbit. It was developed by Bonnie Seeley, who used several rabbit breeds to create this little bundle of fluff.

◀ Even small rabbits can cause disarray in their cages. This Netherland Dwarf has just tipped over its food bowl, which is why such items should be made of earthenware.

→ People of all ages own and enjoy rabbits, but children especially are easily captivated by these charming, lovable pets. In general, rabbit care is not difficult, and a child can actively participate in caring for the family's pet rabbit.

Close-up of a Netherland Dwarf with an ear tattoo. At this time, there are two widely used methods of providing identification for a rabbit. They are tattooing and leg banding. If you are interested in the exhibition side of the rabbit hobby, you should check the regulations of the national rabbit organization for your country. ▶

◀ A trio of American Fuzzy Lops. The body of the American Fuzzy is covered with dense wool, but the ears are coated with regular fur.

SELECTION

The "coat" of the rabbit is another consideration in making your selection. Some breeds have fur coats that are short and dense. Other breeds, such as Angoras, have coats that have the appearance of wooly fleece. If you want one of these wooly breeds, will you or someone else in the family have time to groom it on a regular basis? If you are interested in any of the lop-eared breeds of rabbit, keep in mind that their ears will need extra attention. Loppy ears can be prone to parasitic infestation. Additionally, they are more subject to injuries such as scratches and cuts.

If you want to keep more than one rabbit, then you should choose females (does). Two males (bucks) kept together are more likely to fight. ➥

← Mini Lop. Take your time in choosing your rabbit. The more familiar you are with the breed that interests you the better you will be able to decide if it is the right breed for you.

← American Fuzzy Lop. The amount of food that rabbits consume varies, depending upon the size of a given breed. You may want to take this factor into account when considering the cost of maintaining your pet.

◄ Rabbits can vary somewhat as far as disposition is concerned. Some really enjoy physical contact with humans; others do not and may resist being handled.

SELECTION

The rabbit that you choose should have a nice full coat with no bare patches. As with all other kinds of pets, a rabbit should be carefully examined before you buy it.

American Fuzzy Lop, sable point. Many attractive color patterns can be found among the various breeds of rabbit.

11

SELECTION

Never purchase a rabbit that is under two months of age. Although some baby rabbits are taken away from their mothers at less than this age and they survive, their optimal early development is not as good as rabbits that remain with their mothers for a full two months. When you examine your prospective rabbit, gently stroke it along the back and sides. If the spine and ribs are easily felt, then the animal is likely underweight and should not be considered for purchase.

← Beveren, white. This breed is also available in blue and black.

← Have everything ready for your rabbit before you bring it home. Place the cage in a quiet spot where the rabbit can relax undisturbed.

← A rabbit enjoying a meal of carrot and pelleted food.

SELECTION

Mini Lop. The fur of the rabbit that you purchase should be clean and free of any stains.

Mini Rex. Rex rabbits have beautiful velvety, plush coats.

English Spot. The characteristic nose marking, called a "butterfly," covers the entire whisker bed.

Netherland Dwarf. The rabbit that you choose should be alert and interested in what is going on around it.

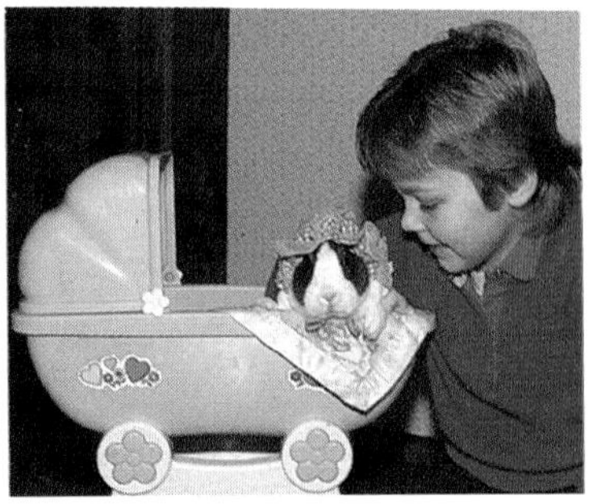

Very young children will need to be taught the correct way to handle their bunny rabbit. Adult supervision is a good idea when a young child and his pet play together.

SELECTION

In general, the average lifespan of domestic rabbits is about six to eight years of age, but there are records of rabbits that have lived up to twelve or more years. Female rabbits that have not been mated tend to be the longest living rabbits.

Silver, fawn. The hallmark of this breed is its beautiful lustrous fur. Silvers are available in several color varieties. ➥

➥ French Angora. A wooly rabbit is beautiful when its wool is in full growth and well groomed.

Your pet shop dealer can supply you with everything that you will need to maintain your rabbit. ➥

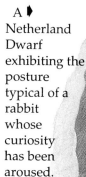

A ➤ Netherland Dwarf exhibiting the posture typical of a rabbit whose curiosity has been aroused.

Mini Lop. Its body markings are known as a broken pattern, which is a combination of any recognized breed color and white. ▶

Dutch rabbits are among the most well-known and quickly recognizable rabbit breeds. In addition to the popular black-and-white version, this breed also comes in several other attractive color patterns.

◀ Rex, chinchilla. A rabbit neither walks nor runs. Instead, it gets around by using the characteristic hippity-hop gait of the lagomorphs. This type of movement is determined by the length of the rabbit's hind legs, which are much longer than the front legs.

HOUSING

There are several considerations to take into account when choosing the type of housing that is just right for your rabbit. It is essential that your rabbit's accommodations be large enough so that your pet can move about in complete comfort. Naturally, the size of your rabbit will determine the size of his house, but even the smallest breed of rabbit should have accommodations that allow it to move about freely.

← Dutch rabbits chowing down. A cardboard box is not suitable for housing, but it can be a fun "toy" in which the rabbits can scamper in and out. (Items made of cardboard are subject to a rabbit's gnawing and thus will have to be discarded after a length of time.)

◀ Mini Lop. The French Lop, Standard Chinchilla, and Netherland Dwarf all contributed to the creation of this breed.

This ▶ hutch features an outdoor play area and an enclosed section in which the rabbit can eat and sleep.

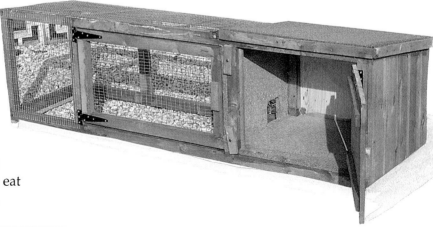

HOUSING

◆ These Mini Rex are being transported to a rabbit show. Thc cage that they are in is obviously too small to serve as permanent housing, but it is fine for purposes of travel.

A Netherland Dwarf that was bred in the UK. Even though the Netherland Dwarf is a very small rabbit, the size of its cage should be *no less* than 24" x 15" x 15". Preferably, it should be even a bit larger than this. ◆

◆ A Creme D'Argent with rather pale coloration. The orange hue of the coat should be bright.

This youngster is checking her pet's water supply. The gravity-fed water bottle that she is holding is ideal for rabbits and many other small mammals, as it prevents an animal from soiling its water supply with droppings or scattered bits of food. ◆

HOUSING

Whatever type of housing that you choose for your rabbit, it should be durable and easy to maintain. Wire cages have much to offer in this respect. They are far sturdier than wood and can better withstand a rabbit's gnawing. Another important feature of the wire cage is that it comes equipped with a pull-out tray on the bottom. The droppings that collect in the tray can be disposed of easily. (By the way, rabbit droppings make a good garden fertilizer.)

← Netherland Dwarf. The head conformation of this breed is noticeably rounder than that of many other rabbit breeds.

◀ A hutch designed to house several rabbit families. A slanted roof will help to prevent the accumulation of rain water, which can rot the wood.

Choose accommodations that allow for easy accessibility to your rabbit and make sure that all doors are equipped with sturdy latches. ▶

← A female bicolored Netherland Dwarf.

▲ A trio of rabbits at play. When playtime is over, white or light-colored rabbits will need a bit more grooming than dark-colored rabbits.

☛ Close-up of a lynx Netherland Dwarf. The erect short ears add to the overall pleasing appearance of the dwarf rabbit.

▲ A European-designed rabbit hutch. Note the wire mesh beneath the hinged wooden-floor sections. Any kind of solid flooring will have to be carefully sanitized on a regular basis to prevent the growth of harmful bacteria.

▲ Rabbits are sometimes given as gifts, especially at the Easter season. A rabbit that is given as a gift should go only to a home where he will really be appreciated and looked after properly.

HOUSING

Whether indoors or outdoors, your rabbit's housing should be located in an area that is well ventilated. The location should be bright but should also afford your pet the opportunity to retreat to the shade when the weather is hot. If outdoors, your rabbit's house must be protected from the elements and from predators.

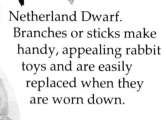

Netherland Dwarf. Branches or sticks make handy, appealing rabbit toys and are easily replaced when they are worn down.

Your rabbit will enjoy the opportunity to play outdoors. For safety's sake, keep it in a confined area so that it can't run away or be harmed by other animals.

A pretty opal agouti Netherland Dwarf.

This Netherland Dwarf is an exhibition rabbit. It is quite used to being touched and handled.

A sable marten Netherland Dwarf.

Once your rabbit gets to know you, it won't be long before he comes to the front of his hutch or cage to greet you at mealtime and see goodies that you have brought for him. Feed your rabbit daily at the same time each day.

Additionally, outdoor housing should have an enclosed area in which your rabbit can comfortably sleep.

← Various breeds of rabbit in a travel cage of an older design. Today, a rabbit keeper can choose from a wide variety of attractive cages and accessories for his pet.

A Dutch rabbit. The fur of this breed is short and dense.

CARE

Caring for your rabbit is a fairly straightforward matter, providing that you follow the basics of good animal husbandry. Of course, the essentials of daily care will vary somewhat, depending upon the breed of rabbit that you own.

← Mini Rex, chinchilla. When purchasing commercial pelleted rabbit food, which is what these rabbits are eating, always check the expiration date on the package. Like many other prepackaged food items, rabbit food has a limited shelf life.

← Jersey Wooly, tortoise. A rabbit is a clean animal and will spend a considerable amount of time grooming itself. Even so, it will benefit greatly from the regular grooming regimen that you establish.

An assortment of Netherland Dwarf rabbits. The color varieties shown here are but a few of the many that exist in this breed.

◀ Jersey Wooly. Always return your rabbit to its cage hind feet first. A rabbit—even a small one—has strong back legs and sharp claws. If startled, it may kick and scratch its handler.

◀ A good way to hold your rabbit. In most instances, a rabbit will enjoy the warmth and security of being cuddled against his human companion.

A pretty Dutch rabbit exhibiting the classic black-and-white color pattern of its breed. ➡

For example, the wool breeds will need more attention to their grooming than will shorthaired rabbits.

Snack time for bunny. Wash all greenfood thoroughly before feeding it to your pet. ➡

CARE

◀ If your rabbit doesn't have regular access to a hard surface such as concrete, its claws may become overgrown and need clipping. Your vet can do this for you.

Mini Rex. The greenfoods that you feed your rabbit should be of the freshest quality.

Good hygiene is one of the essential elements of good husbandry and should be reflected in all aspects of care, from cage cleaning to feeding to grooming. Your pet's cage should be thoroughly cleaned on a weekly basis. If you decide to keep more than one rabbit, you may have to increase the frequency of cage cleaning.

A healthy rabbit will have a good appetite.
◀

◀ This Jersey Wooly is having its claws checked for length. Regularly checking your rabbit for any physical abnormalities can help to prevent the development of serious problems—or at least lessen their severity. Always use a gentle touch when examining your rabbit.

Dutch rabbits enjoying a treat from the garden. Take a few minutes daily to observe your pet while he eats. A change in eating patterns can be a signal that he is not feeling his usual self.

◀ A Netherland Dwarf getting its teeth examined. The upper and lower incisors are visible. In some rabbits, the teeth are misaligned, a condition known as *malocclusion.* Your rabbit probably won't enjoy this procedure, but it is necessary for his good dental health.

➤ A pair of Jersey Woolies, which, basically, are dwarf Angora rabbits. Even though your rabbit is a very adaptable animal, it needs your common-sense care and attention to be a healthy, content pet.

Food and water bowls or bottles should be cleaned daily. Any feeding utensils that become chipped or cracked should be thrown away.

DIET

Your rabbit is a herbivore. That is, he eats only vegetable matter. His relatives in the wild sustain themselves mainly on grasses and various other kinds of vegetation. The pet rabbit is dependent on his owner for a diet that will meet his nutritional needs and help keep him healthy. There are a number of important elements in a rabbit's diet that must be offered in the proper ratio if the animal's metabolic requirements are to be met. They include proteins, carbohydrates, fats, vitamins, and minerals.

← A Netherland Dwarf with an assortment of supplemental foods. The square greenish-colored items are alfalfa hay cubes, which are available at pet shops. Rabbits love them.

Handpicked fresh greens from the garden are a real treat for a rabbit.

← An average-sized gravity-fed water bottle and an array of healthy snacks that any rabbit would enjoy.

Rabbits need roughage in their diets to keep their digestive systems functioning properly. Roughage is an important preventative against gastrointestinal disorders and intestinal blockages. Alfalfa hay is a good source of roughage.

A group of healthy Netherland Dwarfs. Contrary to popular belief—perpetuated in part by famous rabbits such as Peter Rabbit and Bugs Bunny—carrots are not one of the staples of a rabbit's diet. Carrots are not nutritionally complete and should be used only as a supplement to your rabbit's diet.

Rabbits at a community feeder. This arrangement doesn't always work satisfactorily, as the food may not be consumed equally by all of the rabbits.

DIET

A rabbit keeper doesn't have to be an expert in nutri- tion to feed his pet properly. The key to a good rabbit diet is very simple: it's pelleted rabbit food. These specially formulated food mixes, developed by experts in animal nutrition, provide all of the dietary essentials that your rabbit needs. Check with your vet to determine the formula that is best for your rabbit.

A Californian. Your rabbit's size and age will determine the quantity of food that it consumes daily. ➥

An orange Rex buck. It's fine to let your rabbit outdoors, but be sure that he isn't exposed to areas that have been chemically treated. ▼

◄ Remove any leftover greenfoods at the end of each day. This is especially important in hot weather, when food can spoil quickly.

← A black Netherland Dwarf. In addition to size and age, your rabbit's activity level will also determine the quantity of food that is consumed daily. A rabbit that is regularly let out of its cage for play and exercise will likely have a hearty appetite.

← Netherland Dwarfs. Some rabbit keepers prefer alfalfa hay cubes because they are convenient to feed. Others prefer baled hay. Either form will be readily eaten by your rabbit.

← A doe nursing her young. The average size for a rabbit litter is between six and eight, but larger litters have been known to occur.

DIET

▶ Pelleted food should look good and smell good. It should not appear contaminated in any way. There is no exact answer when it comes to the question of how much to feed a rabbit. The best thing that you can do is to monitor your pet at mealtime. If he attacks his food bowl with gusto and eats every single morsel, you can increase the portion. Conversely, if he doesn't eat everything up, you can decrease the amount fed.

Water is an essential part of your rabbit's diet. A rabbit should have access to clean fresh water at all times. If you use a water bottle, be sure that it is not placed directly above the food bowl.

An assortment of food bowls and water containers. The bowl with the clips on the back is an excellent choice. It can be attached to the side of the cage, thereby preventing its contents from being spilled or soiled. There are many useful cage accessories available for rabbits.

A proper diet is one of the essential elements of a rabbit's good health. Pictured is an English Spot, which is known in some parts of Europe as the English Butterfly.

Greenfoods are a supplement to the main diet of pelleted food. They should not be fed to bunnies under the age of five to six months because they can cause problems in the digestive tract. (Remember, when feeding greenfoods to adult rabbits, serve small quantities.)

Sometimes these bottles release occasional droplets of water, which can make the food soggy, or even spoil it.

An adorable pair of Dwarf Hotots.

DIET

As far as greenfoods go, rabbits can vary in their preferences. Finding out which ones your rabbit likes best is simply a matter of trial and error. Changes in diet should always be made gradually to prevent the occurence of diarrhea, or scours.

◆ Rabbits and other small mammals such as guinea pigs like lettuce, but it has no nutritional value and can cause diarrhea.

The hay that you ◆ provide for your rabbit should be fresh and clean. It should be changed frequently.

You can give your rabbit a small treat in ◆ between meals.

◆ This mixed-breed pregnant doe is preparing a nest made of soft fur that she has pulled from her chest and stomach. A few bits of straw have gotten entangled in the fur.

➥ An assortment of edible wild plants: dandelion (left), mallow (right), and plantain (bottom).

➥ All of these plants are poisonous: poison hemlock (left), jimsonweed (center), and water hemlock. If you are interested in collecting wild plant foods for your rabbit, you should first invest in a plant identification book.

A pair of Dutch rabbits about to start grazing on the grass. ➥

HEALTH

A rabbit that is properly cared for hopefully will enjoy a good state of health. Many of the illnesses that strike rabbits are the result of unsanitary living conditions, improper care, or poor diet. Good husbandry is very important in keeping your rabbit healthy. Make sure the cage tray is emptied daily and clean the entire cage once a week. Remove uneaten food daily.

◄ A Rex rabbit. The more familiar you are with your rabbit's behavior, the easier it will be for you to detect when he is not feeling well.

This Netherland Dwarf is suffering from dermatitis, for which a veterinarian can prescribe medication. Always wash your hands after handling a rabbit that has any kind of health problem.

Bright eyes, a dry nose, and a full coat are all signs of good health in a ▶ rabbit.

HEALTH

◀ Two of the large rabbit breeds: a New Zealand and a Flemish Giant. Cramped quarters cause stress, which can have a direct effect on a rabbit's health. This is true for every breed of rabbit, regardless of its size.

Psoroptes cuniculi, the ear mite that causes psoroptic ➴ ear mange.

Rabbits can fall prey to a number of parasitic ◀ infestations. This rabbit has a bad case of psoroptic ear mange. The best way to help prevent such a problem is to regularly inspect your rabbit and keep his housing as clean as you can.

The bent front paws on this rabbit could be a symptom of rickets. A rabbit that is fed the ➴ proper diet has little risk of being stricken with this condition.

◀ A nice collection of Netherland Dwarfs, all of which are under the age of five months.

HEALTH

Unfortunately, even with the best of care, a rabbit can sometimes become ill. Stomach disorders, many of which are accompanied by diarrhea, can be serious— sometimes even fatal—and should be treated as soon as they are detected. A rabbit that has diarrhea should be taken off all greenfoods

← Dwarf Hotot. Small breeds can be safely held in this manner. Note that leg movement is restricted, which prevents the handler from being scratched.

immediately and given an anti-diarrheal preparation. Some experienced rabbit keepers regularly treat their stock with sulfaquinoxaline as a preventative against coccidiosis, a digestive-tract infection that is not uncommon in rabbits.

← A sick rabbit should never be kept with ones that are healthy.

A rabbit suffering from coccidiosis, an illness that is particularly hard on young rabbits. One of the symptoms of coccidiosis is an overall rough appearance to the fur. ←

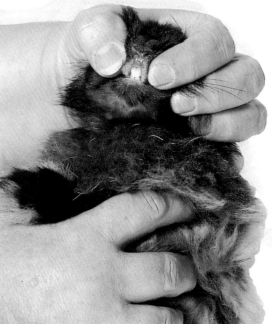

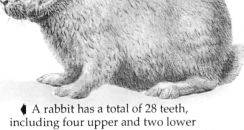

◄ A rabbit has a total of 28 teeth, including four upper and two lower incisors. The upper incisors are paired in twos. The smaller pair is set behind the larger pair.

This rabbit has an advanced case of ringworm, a skin disease that can be transmitted to humans. Many domestic pets are susceptible to ringworm.

A Dutch rabbit. In general, rabbits are hardy animals and can live healthy lives if they are cared for properly.

For those who are just getting into rabbits, it is best to check with a vet regarding the treatment of any health problem—internal or external.

Rabbit pals at play. If you keep a pair of rabbits, it is possible that they will bond more closely with each other than with you.

REGULAR RABBITS

In the world of rabbits, the breeds are categorized into three groups: fancy, fur, and meat. In this book, however, the breeds have been grouped somewhat differently to make it easier for the reader who is just beginning to learn the basics about rabbits:

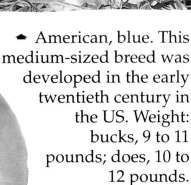

◆ American, blue. This medium-sized breed was developed in the early twentieth century in the US. Weight: bucks, 9 to 11 pounds; does, 10 to 12 pounds.

◆ American, blue and white. The blue variety has blue-gray eyes. The white variety has pink eyes.

American Sable. In this breed, the head conformation of the doe is more refined than that of the buck. Weight: bucks, 7 to 9 pounds; does, 8 to 10 pounds.

REGULAR RABBITS

regular rabbits (all non-wooly rabbits over three pounds), wooly (Angora) rabbits, and the littlest rabbits (those whose ideal weight is three pounds or under). The only exception to this grouping is the Jersey Wooly, whose ideal weight is also three pounds but which, by virtue of its Angora-like quality, has been placed with its larger wooly cousins.

◆ When the American Sable is viewed in reflected light, its brown eyes give off a ruby-red glow. Another distinguishing feature of this breed is its rich sepia brown color, which varies in its intensity on different parts of the animal's body.

The American Sable has an undercoat that is dense, soft, and fine. Dispersed throughout the undercoat is an abundance of rather coarse guard hairs. These guard hairs act as a protectant for the undercoat. The fur, overall, should be uniform in length and well balanced.

Belgian Hare. Though it is called a hare, it is, indeed, a rabbit. Many years ago, it was the most popular rabbit in the fancy. The body of the Belgian Hare is narrow and long in appearance. Its long legs enable it to move about quickly. An outstanding feature of the breed is its beautiful color, which is a rich deep red of a chestnut or tan hue. Weight: bucks and does, 6 to 9 ½ pounds.

REGULAR RABBITS

Thanks to successful selective breeding throughout the many years that rabbits have been kept in captivity, a large number of rabbit breeds have been developed, and more are being developed all the time. They come in a great variety of sizes and an even greater variety of colors and patterns.

▲ Beveren. This breed was developed in Beveren, Belgium. For a while, it was utilized as a source of meat in England during World War I. The Beveren has a medium-long body with shoulders that appear firm and strong. Weight: bucks, 8 to 10 pounds; does, 9 to 11 pounds.

The ears of the Belgian Hare are narrow and long. They are carried in a backward slope. The eyes are large and bold.

◀

REGULAR RABBITS

A blue Beveren. The body of a good specimen when viewed from the side will present a clearly defined arch.

The Beveren's fur is dense and glossy. Ideally, the length of the fur is between 1" and 1½" inches. The "V"-shaped ear carriage is characteristic of the breed.

Californian. Three other rabbit breeds contributed to the creation of the Californian: the Himalayan, the Chinchilla, and the New Zealand. Californians have pure white bodies with Himalayan-like markings, which, ideally, should be as close to black as possible. Weight: bucks, 8 to 10 pounds; does, 8½ to 10½ pounds.

The body of the Californian is medium in length. The well-rounded hindquarters are broad and well fleshed. They are somewhat deeper and wider than the shoulders.

REGULAR RABBITS

In addition to being a highly popular pet and exhibition animal, the rabbit has been utilized extensively in laboratory research in the fields of genetics and nutrition.

Additionally, the rabbit has been useful in scientific research devoted to new and improved treatments for diseases in humans.

Champagne D'Argent. This breed is named for the Champagne region of France, where it originated, and for the silverish appearance of its fur. (In French, *argent* means silver.) French peasants originally used it for both its meat and fur. Weight: bucks, 9 to 11 pounds; does, 9½ to 12 pounds.

◄ Checkered Giant. This attractive breed comes in two color varieties: black and blue. Ideally, the markings on the sides of the body are well balanced and well proportioned. Weight: bucks, 11 pounds or more; does, 12 pounds or more.

This is the proper show stance for a Checkered Giant. The body is carried sufficiently above the ground and forms a full arch.

Chinchilla, Giant. This breed and the other breeds of Chinchilla get their name from the wild chinchilla, whose fur color and pattern they resemble. Weight: bucks, 12 pounds or more; does, 13 pounds or more.

Chinchilla, Standard. Chinchilla rabbits have long been prized for their lovely fur, which in texture is dense and fine. Weight: bucks, 5 to 7 pounds; does, 5½ to 7½ pounds.

Chinchilla fur is also bright and glossy in appearance. The beautiful coloration is due, in part, to *ticking,* the term used to describe the long guard hairs that are interspersed throughout the fur. These guard hairs are of a color that is different from that of the body fur or underwool.

REGULAR RABBITS

It's easy to understand why rabbits have so much appeal as pets: they are very adaptable; they are not plagued to any large degree with breed-related problems; and they have little tendency to be aggressive with humans.

◄Cinnamon. The rust or cinnamon color of this breed is enhanced by smoke-gray ticking on various parts of the body. Weight: bucks, $8\,^1/_2$ to $10\,^1/_2$ pounds; does, 9 to 11 pounds.

The Cinnamon has a medium-long body. The well roundedness of the hindquarters, which are a bit wider and deeper than the shoulders, carries into the loin and back. ▶

◄A well-marked Cinnamon will have a clearly defined dark mask on its nose. In addition, it will have dark eye circles that are small and distinct in appearance.

Creme D'Argent. The outstanding feature of this breed is its beautifully colored fur, which is a pleasing shade of orange. The Creme D'Argent is a medium-sized rabbit. Weight: bucks, 8 to $10\,^1/_2$ pounds; does, $8\,^1/_2$ to 11 pounds. ▶

REGULAR RABBITS

Dutch. This breed, believed to have originated in Holland, is one of the oldest fancy rabbit breeds. Weight: bucks and does, 3 $\frac{1}{2}$ to 5 $\frac{1}{2}$ pounds.

The white area on the body just behind the shoulders is called a *saddle*. In a good Dutch specimen, the saddle's line of demarcation —where the color begins—will be straight and even. The white area on the head is called a blaze. It should be medium wide and wedge shaped.

Flemish Giant. This breed originated in Europe. While Flemish Giants are large and heavy boned, they should not be overly fat or flabby. Balance and proportion are two important considerations when assessing the quality of this breed. Weight: bucks, 13 pounds or more; does, 14 pounds or more.

English Spot. As its name implies, this breed originated in England. Its distinguishing feature is its body markings. The fur of this breed is short, dense, and lustrous in appearance. Weight: bucks and does, 5 to 8 pounds.

REGULAR RABBITS

As is true for other kinds of pet animals, some rabbit breeds are rarer than others and can be found only at very large rabbit shows. In the US, the largest rabbit organization is the American Rabbit Breeders Association (ARBA). In the UK, it is the British Rabbit Council.

▲ Florida White. This compact, cobby rabbit was originally developed to be used in research. Its hindquarters and shoulders are well developed, and it is deep and firm in the loin. The Florida White has pure white fur and pink eyes. Weight: Bucks and does, 4 to 6 pounds.

▲Harlequin. This unusual-looking breed of rabbit originated in France. It made its first appearance at a show in Paris in 1887. Weight: bucks, 6 $1/2$ to 9 pounds; does, 7 to 9 $1/2$ pounds.

Harlequins are medium-boned, well-muscled rabbits. They are firmly fleshed, not flabby. Their finely textured fur is soft and dense.

REGULAR RABBITS

The stance of this Harlequin is that typical of a rabbit grooming itself. This photo clearly illustrates the highly distinctive checkered coloration of this breed.

This is a magpie harlequin. In this variety, the golden orange or golden fawn coloration is replaced by white. Color combinations are as follows: black and white; lavender blue and white; dove gray and white; dark chocolate and white.

Havana. The ancestry of this breed, which first appeared in Europe, is uncertain. By the beginning of the twentieth century, the Havana had achieved popularity in various parts of Europe, and this trend soon continued in the US. In overall appearance, the Havana is short in body length and broad and medium short in the conformation of the head. Weight: bucks, 4 $\frac{1}{2}$ to 6 $\frac{1}{2}$ pounds.

REGULAR RABBITS

If you want to see firsthand the many breeds of rabbit that are available to better decide which breed interests you the most, you might want to consider attending a rabbit show. Additionally, you can familiarize yourself with the rabbit standards, which are "pictures in words" of what ideal breed specimens look like.

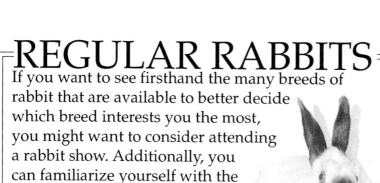

Himalayan. This internationally known breed has been known under a variety of different names throughout its history, including the "Chinese black-nosed rabbit" and the "Russian rabbit." The Himmy's long cylindrical body presents a marked difference in appearance from that of many of the other rabbit breeds. Weight: bucks and does, $2\,^1/_2$ to $4\,^1/_2$ pounds.

Hotot. This breed originated in France, where it is known as the Blanc De Hotot. The body of the Hotot is thickset and well rounded. The distinguishing feature of this breed is the "spectacles," or eyebands, that encircle the eyes. Weight: bucks, 8 to 10 pounds; does, 9 to 11 pounds.

Lop, English. Believed to be another of the oldest domesticated breeds of rabbit, this impressive-looking rabbit bears the title "King of the Fancy" in Europe. Weight: bucks, 9 pounds or more; does, 10 pounds or more.

Ear length, measured from tip to tip, should be at least 21 inches. Lengths of over 30 inches have been recorded. In assessing an English Lop, overall balance and quality are more important factors than ear length itself.

◗ Lop, French. As you might guess by looking at the ears, the English Lop was one of the breeds used in the French Lop's development. French Lops are real "people" rabbits: they are affectionate and amusing, and they enjoy the attention of their human companions. Weight: bucks, 10 pounds or more; does, 11 pounds or more.

◖French Lops are massive and thickset in appearance. Many fanciers of this breed claim that these rabbits make wonderful pets.

Lop, Mini. This breed originated in Germany, where it is known as the *Klein Widder,* (Little Hanging Ear). Due to the considerable degree of inbreeding used to create Mini Lops, they can suffer problems with their ears and teeth, as well as overall size. Weight: bucks and does, 4 1/2 to 6 1/2 pounds.

The coloration of the Mini Lop is of one of two types: solid (self) or broken pattern (white in combination with another color).◗

REGULAR RABBITS

If you select a purebred rabbit, you will have a pretty good idea as to how big it will be as an adult. With a crossbred rabbit, however, the results are very often less predictable—especially if you don't know what the parents look like. Purebreds and crossbreds can make equally fine pets.

◆ In the past, some Mini Lop breeders decreased their rabbits' food portions to keep their rabbits small, which is a practice to be discouraged. The general size of any rabbit breed is a matter of genetics, not diet.

▲ The Mini Lop is thickset and balanced in general overall appearance. Its shoulders have good depth and are well filled.

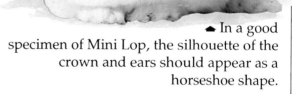

▲ In a good specimen of Mini Lop, the silhouette of the crown and ears should appear as a horseshoe shape.

◆ Head study of a Mini Rex. This breed has the same velvety plush fur as that of its bigger cousin the Rex. Weight: bucks, 3 to 4 $\frac{1}{4}$ pounds; does, 3 $\frac{1}{4}$ to 4 $\frac{1}{2}$ pounds.

REGULAR RABBITS

The fur of the Rex rabbits is quite dense and has a lustrous appearance. Ideally, the length and texture of it should be uniform over the entire body.

New Zealand, black. The New Zealand is well-known as a meat producer. Additionally, its fur is utilized commercially as well. Weight: Bucks, 9 to 11 pounds; does, 10 to 12 pounds.

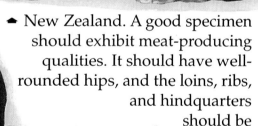

New Zealand. A good specimen should exhibit meat-producing qualities. It should have well-rounded hips, and the loins, ribs, and hindquarters should be well filled.

New Zealand, red. The red variety is a bright shade of reddish sorrel. (The color of the belly can be somewhat lighter.) The coloring around the eyes is not a true eyeband but rather the result of thinner fur.

REGULAR RABBITS

Even though rabbits have a long-standing association with man, the fancy rabbit as we know it today did not emerge on the exhibition scene until the early part of the nineteenth century. It has continued to grow in popularity ever since.

Palomino. This breed, which was developed in the US, comes in two color varieties: golden and lynx. Weight: bucks, 8 to 10 pounds; does, 9 to 11 pounds. ◆

◀The Palomino has a moderately long body. Its shoulders and hindquarters are well developed. The top of the body should form a smooth arc that begins at the nape of the neck. The arc then rises gradually along the back and continues down over the hindquarters.

◆ The Palomino's medium-length head, carried erectly, is set close on the shoulders. The ears, carried together, should be in proportion to the body and head.

Rex. Members of this breed have a separate standard for their fur, which is quite different from rabbits with normal fur. Rex fur is quite short and stands upright from the body. Weight: bucks, 7 $^1/_2$ to 9 $^1/_2$ pounds; does, 8 to 10 $^1/_2$ pounds. ◗

REGULAR RABBITS

◀ A good specimen of Rex will be balanced and well proportioned. Rex rabbits are medium-boned. Their backs and sides are broad and firm, and their hindquarters are smooth and well rounded.

Rhinelander. This breed, which is of German origin, is quite popular in Europe. It has been raised for its fur as well as for its meat. Weight: bucks, 6 $^1/_2$ to 9 $^1/_2$ pounds; does, 7 to 10 pounds. ▶

The hallmark of the Rhinelander is the lovely contrast of black and golden-orange against white. In all of the marked areas on the body, the colors should be evenly distributed and well balanced. ▶

REGULAR RABBITS

Satin. This breed, which was developed in the US, is quickly recognizable because of the lovely sheen of its fur. Weight: bucks, $8\frac{1}{2}$ to $10\frac{1}{2}$ pounds; does, 9 to 11 pounds.

This pair of Satins displays two of the many colors that are available in their breed. The Satin rabbit has its own standard by which its fur is judged.

Today, the keeping of pet rabbits is more popular than ever before, and no doubt the rabbit hobby will continue to grow even more as those seeking a good pet learn more about all of the advantages that these delightful animals have to offer.

The uniqueness of the Satin's fur is the result of a mutation. The transparent quality of the hair shells causes them to reflect light and creates the fur's satin-like appearance.

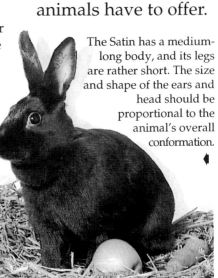
The Satin has a medium-long body, and its legs are rather short. The size and shape of the ears and head should be proportional to the animal's overall conformation.

A red Satin. Note the erect ear carriage, which is characteristic of this breed.

REGULAR RABBITS

◀ Silver. The attractive appearance of this breed is created by the silvering in the fur, which is quite short in length. Weight: bucks and does, 4 to 7 pounds.

Silver Marten. This breed is the result of a cross between a Chinchilla rabbit and a Tan rabbit. The striking color contrast of the fur is due to silver-tipped guard hairs. Weight: bucks, 6 to 8 $^1/_2$ pounds; does, 7 to 9 $^1/_2$ pounds. ◀

◄ A good specimen of a Silver Marten will have an even distribution of silvering with no stray white hairs.

The coloration of the Tan is enhanced by the quality of the fur, which is glossy and lustrous.
◀

◀ Tan. This breed derives its name from its deep, rich tan color, which is primarily on the underside of the body. Weight: bucks, 4 to 5 $^1/_2$ pounds; does, 4 to 6 pounds.

WOOLY RABBITS

The crowning glory of the wooly rabbit is its elegant coat, which creates a beautiful appearance. The wooly rabbit's heritage can be traced back, in part, to what was once known simply as the Angora, which supposedly originated in Turkey. Today, there are four separate breeds that have the word "Angora" as part of their name.

◆ American Fuzzy Lop. Members of this breed are cobby and short. They should be of good depth starting at the shoulders and continuing back to the hindquarters, which should be well rounded. Weight: bucks and does, not more than 4 pounds.

◆ The ears of the American Fuzzy should be full and well-rounded at the tips. Ideally, the ear openings are held close to the jaws.

◆ This pair of American Fuzzies exhibits two of the color groups recognized in this breed. The wool of the American Fuzzy Lop should be uniform in its density. As is true for the other wool breeds as well, wool that is very thin or matted is undesirable.

◆ The American Fuzzy Lop is one of the newer breeds in the world of rabbits. Its cute loppy-eared, wooly appearance and diminutive size are qualities that are attracting the interest of a number of would-be rabbit owners.

Angora, French. This breed is somewhat larger than its English cousin and does not carry head furnishings. This is a firm-fleshed rabbit with hindquarters that are well filled. When looked at from the side, the French Angora appears oval in shape. Weight: bucks and does, 7½ to 10 ½ pounds. ➥

← Angora, English. The impressive appearance of this breed is accentuated by the tassels and fringes on its ears and the growths of wool, called "furnishings," on the top and and sides of the head. When the English Angora is being exhibited, it should be round and fluffy in appearance. Weight: bucks, 5 to 7 pounds; does, 5 to 7½ pounds.

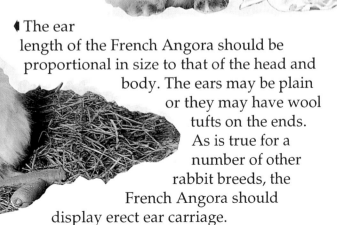

◄ The ear length of the French Angora should be proportional in size to that of the head and body. The ears may be plain or they may have wool tufts on the ends. As is true for a number of other rabbit breeds, the French Angora should display erect ear carriage.

WOOLY RABBITS

The length, density, and texture of wool varies among rabbits of the wool breeds. For example, the Satin Angora's wool is finer than normal Angora wool. At rabbit shows, judges will blow into the wool in order to assess its overall density.

Angora, Giant. This beautiful rabbit, which comes only in white, is distinguished by the abundant tassles and fringes on its ears. Angora wool is of great commercial value in the manufacturing of garments. An Angora in good condition can yield up to 12 ounces of wool annually. Weight: bucks, 8½ pounds or more; does, 9 pounds or more.

Angora, Satin. This breed of rabbit is distinguished by the lovely quality of its wool, which is silky and shiny—quite different from that of the other wool breeds. Weight: bucks and does, 6 pounds or more.

The unique quality of the Satin Angora's wool is actually due to the transparency of the hair shafts, which can reflect light. The beautiful condition of the wool enhances all of the colors in which this breed is available.

WOOLY RABBITS

➥ Jersey Wooly. This relatively recent addition to the rabbit fancy is enjoying a steady rise in popularity. The goal of the breeder who developed the Jersey Wooly was to create a small wooly pet rabbit with good "type" (distinguishable characteristics). Today, the Jersey Wooly is available in five color groups. Weight: bucks and does, 3½ pounds or less.

A tortie Jersey Wooly. As is true for a number of other wool rabbit breeds, the coloration of the head and extremities can be markedly more pronounced than the body color. This is due to the length of the wool, which tends to "soften" a given color. ▶

◀ Head study of a Jersey Wooly. As you might have guessed, the Netherland Dwarf was instrumental in the creation of this breed. This is readily apparent in the well-rounded head and short, erect ears. The body of the Jersey Wooly is compact and short-coupled in appearance.

THE LITTLEST ONES

Dwarf rabbits present no more problems to the rabbit keeper than do any of the other rabbit breeds. This was not always so. In the early days of their development, they were beset by problems such as nervous temperament, malocclusion, and poor breeding records. Conscientious, committed breeders worked and succeeded in remedying these situations.

◆ Britannia Petite. This breed is the American counterpart to the Polish (rabbit) as seen in the UK. It has white fur and red eyes. It is believed by many to be the original type of dwarf rabbit and was exhibited as long ago as 1884 in Britain. The Britannia Petite is a lively, spirited little rabbit. Weight: bucks and does, maximum 2½ pounds.

Dwarf Hotot. This breed, which is of German origin, bears the same markings as those of its larger cousin. Its size and appearance are the result of mixing Hotot and dwarf genes. Weight: bucks and does, maximum 3¼ pounds. ▶

◆ The Dwarf Hotot is a compact rabbit with well-rounded hindquarters. Its white fur is fine and soft and imparts a lustrous appearance. The Dwarf Hotot made its debut in the US around 1981 and was given full breed recognition in 1983.

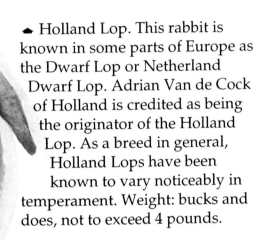

← In overall general appearance, the Holland Lop is thickset and compact. The thick, full ears, rounded at the tips, should be in balance with the body and head.

← Holland Lop. This rabbit is known in some parts of Europe as the Dwarf Lop or Netherland Dwarf Lop. Adrian Van de Cock of Holland is credited as being the originator of the Holland Lop. As a breed in general, Holland Lops have been known to vary noticeably in temperament. Weight: bucks and does, not to exceed 4 pounds.

← Netherland Dwarf, blue tan. These rabbits are the smallest rabbit breed in the world. They have been used to develop a number of other rabbit breeds. Weight: not more than 2½ pounds.

← It is not known for certain exactly where the Netherland Dwarf first originated, but it is likely that the Polish (as seen in Europe) was used in its creation.

THE LITTLEST ONES

In addition to its status as a popular pet, the Netherland Dwarf has the distinction of being the most popular show rabbit in the US. It also has a large following in the UK and Europe.

◆ Blue silver marten Netherland Dwarfs. In some parts of Europe, this breed is known as the European Pole.

◆ Lynx Netherland Dwarf. These rabbits appeared in England around 1948 and were well received in the fancy. They were first seen in the US in 1969 and enjoyed the same instant success.

◆ A very alert Netherland Dwarf. Members of this breed are active little rabbits.

◆ "Round" is a good word to use when describing the appearance of the Netherland Dwarf. This is true for both the body and head.

THE LITTLEST ONES

These young Netherland Dwarfs, all under the age of six months, are not of show quality, but they can make very good pets. ➤

◀ American-bred Polish, blue-eyed white and black. The Polish is a small, compact rabbit. Members of this breed are known for their lively temperaments. Weight: bucks and does, not more than 3 ½ pounds.

◄ This inquisitive pair of Netherland Dwarfs exhibits the ear carriage typical of their breed.

The Polish as seen in Great Britain. It is bred in a number of attractive colors. This rabbit is exhibiting a nice show stance. ▶

◀ Body study of a Polish (American bred).

INDEX

Page numbers in **boldface** refer to illustrations.

Alfalfa hay cubes, **26**, **29**
American, **38**
American Fuzzy Lop, **56**
American Rabbit Breeders
Association, 46
American Sable, **38,39**
Angora, English, **57**
Angora, French, **57**
Angora, Giant, **58**
Angora, Satin, **58**
Belgian Hare, **39,40**
Beveren, **40,41**
British Rabbit Council, 46
Brittania Petite, **60**
"Butterfly", **13**
Cages, **7**, 18
Californian, **41**
Champagne D'Argent, **42**
Checkered Giant, **42**
Chinchilla, Giant, **43**
Chinchilla, Standard, **43**
Cinnamon, **44**
Claws, **24**, **25**
Coccidiosis, 36
Creme D'Argent, **44**
Dermatitis, **34**
Diarrhea, 32, 36
Diet, **26**, 28
Dutch, **45**
Dwarf Hotot, **60**
English Spot, **45**
Flemish Giant, **45**
Florida White, **46**
Greenfoods, **24**, **31**, 32, 36

Handling, **23**
Harlequin, **46,47**
Havana, **47**
Health, 34
Himalayan, **48**
Hotot, **48**
Jersey Wooly, **59**
Lifespan, 14
Lop, English, **48**
Lop, French, **49**
Lop, Holland, **61**
Lop, Mini, **49,50**
Mini Rex, **50**
Netherland Dwarf, **61,62,63**
New Zealand, **51**
Oryctolagus cuniculus, 4
Palomino, **52**
Polish, **63**
Psoroptes cuniculi, **35**
Psoroptic ear mange, **35**
Rex, **52,53**
Rhinelander, **53**
Ringworm, 37
Satin, **54**
Seeley, Bonnie, 8
Silver, **55**
Silver Marten, **55**
Standards, 48
Sulfaquinoxaline, 36
Tan, **55**
Teeth, 4, **25**, **36**
Water, 30